Cloud Computing For Business

How smart SMEs are using the benefits of cloud computing to slash costs, work flexibly and dominate their market (and how you can too)

Chris Brownlee

Cloud Computing For Business

First published in the United Kingdom in 2015 by Chris Brownlee.

Design and layout by Hello Genius Limited.

Dedicated to those who consider themselves not to be 'everyone'

Contents

Introduction

Businesses have never had it so tough.

Alongside one of the fiercest competitive environments in a generation, painfully high levels of bureaucracy and red tape and the ever-present threat of economic downturn, staying afloat - let alone growing a business - remains a serious challenge.

Yet we live in a world where technology is worshipped as a means to make our business lives better.

As in the consumer world, new technologies are touted as our saviours; they'll drive more customers into our business, generate more sales and help our businesses become bigger and more profitable.

That's the theory.

The everyday reality for many businesses is somewhat different.

The advent of email and the web was supposed to take pressure off as an alternative to the telephone and fax machine. Transactions and deals were supposed to have become easier and more fluid without bothersome human interaction slowing things down.

Our desktop computers were intended to be our Man Fridays... there to help us march out into the world of commerce armed with all the processing power and communication tools we needed.

So why do we find ourselves sitting behind our desks regularly cursing at our computer monitors?

Why do we have a mounting suspicion when people put deadlines and cost caps on IT projects?

Why has the time-worn phrase "have you turned it off and on again?" - so beloved of IT support operatives and dreaded by beleaguered employees - become such a rally cry for those who would suggest technology has done little for the execution of our everyday business?

You'd be hard-pressed to argue technology hasn't been responsible for the huge growth of giants such as Wal-Mart and dominance of online businesses such as Amazon. But the truth is technology has not served many small and medium-sized businesses as well as it could have.

The gains in time and effort made by the adoption of technologies such as email and web services is tempered by the loss of thousands of productive hours. This is time spent dealing with a combined onslaught of security issues, IT firefighting and maintenance, loss of data with a major impact on staff productivity, both intended and accidental. And not forgetting the open stable door of allowing disgruntled employees a direct line to your most valuable company data and information at the click of a button should they decide to act maliciously.

My view, however, is that technology isn't the issue.

Unrealistic expectations about what technology can do within a business and the extent to which it can help a business grow have been the cause of many IT disappointments.

Technology manufacturers and IT providers shoulder some of the blame in their eagerness to persuade SMEs of the need to adopt office-based technology designed to help their business. What is rarely mentioned in the sales pitch is the expertise and experience needed to make IT function effectively within the workplace, on top of the commitment needed to maintain, update and upgrade systems to keep the business moving.

That's where my business has stepped in.

As managing director of technology services company Worknet, we've helped businesses harness technology the way it is supposed to be used within a business. We help grow your business and allow you to focus on your core competencies: attracting new customers and servicing your existing ones.

With businesses struggling to cope with serious IT technical issues, security challenges and the threat of their data and systems from cyber hacking, now is the time to re-assess what technology is for and whether there is an alternative to in-house IT networks.

Fortunately, the alternative is here: cloud computing.

The arrival of cloud computing - or The Cloud, as it's been popularly branded - heralds an opportunity for SMEs to take control of their IT systems once and for all.

The UK cloud computing market alone was set to be worth £6.1 billion in 2014.[1]

Already 18% of SMEs in the UK were using cloud services in 2014 and a further 30% plan to use them within in the next 12 months.[2]

Although the majority of businesses taking advantage of cloud services in the UK are software companies, there are plentiful opportunities for companies of every size in all sectors to derive benefits from The Cloud.

Cloud computing offers the chance to take management of all your business's IT issues away while remaining fully in control. Cloud computing can also offer:

- Better cost planning and forecasting

- The highest levels of resilience

- Built-in disaster recovery

- Vastly improved security and back-up

- Greater scaleability

- Remote and out-of-office working

In this book, my aim is to provide an overview of the problems faced by SMEs dealing with technology and how these are being overcome by cloud computing technologies. Furthermore, I'll demonstrate how you can apply these

---

[1] TechMarketView

[2] 'Information Communications Technology (ICT) in the UK: investment opportunities' 19/02/2014 *UK Trade & Investment, gov.uk*

technologies in your own business and begin to reap the benefits cloud computing offers.

I've first-hand experience seeing how businesses struggle with the day-to-day issues of technology. I understand exactly how coping with an email system which fails at the very moment you need it or a server which breaks down during an intensely busy period can seriously affect your business.

In my opinion, technology should work <u>for</u> you, not the other way around.

And in the following pages, I aim to demonstrate why I believe cloud computing is the solution SMEs have been promised but have not - so far - enjoyed.

Let's explore The Cloud

Chris Brownlee
Managing Director, Worknet Ltd

Marlow, United Kingdom

FREE DOWNLOAD - Discover how smart SMEs are leaving behind traditional IT and using cloud technology to make their business more reliable, flexible and secure to help grow.

Go to www.worknet.co.uk/smart to download your free 8-page guide 'Time to ditch the server?'

Part I
Introducing
The Cloud

Time to ditch the server?

Three growing trends which show why in-house IT isn't working

There's a revolution quietly going on with how small and medium-sized businesses think about technology. For too long, businesses tolerated poor performing IT systems which promised to deliver and instead diverted time, money and resource away from their core business function.

For many businesses, when it comes to technology their only experience is 'fire-fighting'. Constantly and repetitively dealing with the same issues every day saps valuable time and energy which could be used to move the business forward. The feeling is that your IT is almost a hindrance but this is a reality affecting far more UK businesses than it should.

And it goes deeper than day-to-day issues. Poorly performing technology has the side-effect of making a business vulnerable to a number of external pressures, some of which could even close the business permanently.

Here, I explore three key trends UK companies are having to deal with right now from a technology perspective. In doing so, it also highlights just why the in-house model of IT is actively causing more problems than it is solves.

1. IT issues are diverting more time and resource from productive work than ever

Even in 2015, there are companies who still find themselves dealing with routine IT problems. It's a worrying statistic that IT managers find themselves spending up to 70% of their productive hours dealing with routine IT problems rather than being able to focus on using IT to move the business forward.[3]

Among the technology issues businesses face are:

- The 'IT system' going down, particularly when at full capacity.

- Constantly requiring time-consuming manual updates or costly upgrades.

- Incompatibility issues between different operating systems and programmes.

- Having to find 'workarounds' to make your IT system fit to how you do your job.

- Needing to upgrade computers to cope with new resource-hungry solutions and applications.

---

[3] Cisco

- Manually having to back-up data onto hard drives, disks and tapes.

- Having to move files and data insecurely using disks and USB sticks whenever users would like to work remotely- and then working out how to update the original files.

Businesses find themselves struggling with issues which hinder their performance and damage their ability to not only service their customers effectively but grow the business. Any activity which takes your business away from its core purpose, quite simply, reduces your ability to grow.

When did 'just working as it should' become the aspiration for the way a business's IT should be? It seems incredible that, in 2015, many UK businesses don't expect more of their technology investment.

Research backs up British business's lack of faith in IT. According to a survey by the Epson Business Council, only 51% of UK firms thought IT would be integral to driving their business, compared with 76% of French and German firms.

In the mass of IT problems that businesses face on a day-to-day basis, it has been forgotten that technology should facilitate your company operations.

It should seamlessly integrate to offer unlimited and reliable access to all your applications, communications and, most importantly, should run in the background with no issues or problems. In other words, as a bare minimum, you shouldn't have to consciously think about IT issues;

your system should be working with minimal intervention and little 'downtime'.

The only time your IT infrastructure should move front of mind is when you are using it to leverage increasing opportunities for growth.

2. Hackers targeting vulnerable and small businesses

Cybercrime is an issue which the public perceives affects only government departments, big business and credit card holders. For most business owners, they don't even realise it's a serious problem to consider until it's too late...

The scourge of cybercrime costs small businesses up to £785 million per year, according to a report from the Federation of Small Business (FSB) in May 2013. And the cost and scale of the problem is set to rise.

An incredible 41% of FSB members had been victims of cybercrime in the preceding 12 months, with 20% suffering from virus infections, the most common form of attack for businesses in the UK. Most worryingly, almost 20% take no steps to protect themselves from attack.

Although many businesses undertake some form of protection against cyber-based activity with 36% claiming to regularly install updates and 60% regularly updating their virus scanning software, these can require constant monitoring and immediate action to plug the holes through which hackers can attack – especially where a server is involved.

The truth is smaller businesses are a soft target for hackers. It's far easier to target a business without dedicated information security specialists working 24 hours a day to keep these attacks at bay.

It is understandable why small businesses struggle to keep on top of technology issues with the many threats at their door. Yet, it's unlikely many companies have the resource to enact comprehensive information security policies. With attacks on network from cyber criminals set to increase, securing your network will become an essential part of staying in business.

Businesses with an in-house IT person will be able to undertake some of these. However, most businesses simply do not have this resource.

As the vulnerability to cyber attack has increased so do the demands placed upon businesses to counteract the avalanche of viruses, spam alerts and hacking issues which go hand-in-hand with operating in an online environment, it is no wonder so many businesses have turned away from in-house IT infrastructure and 'doing it all themselves'.

The outsourcing of an entire IT function is now commonplace in many fast-growth businesses and companies where human resource is limited and needs to be directed towards productivity, rather than dealing with operational issues.

The idea of outsourcing the entire management of IT to a dedicated specialist no longer fills businesses with dread, particularly as the IT and security needs have tipped the balance and proved too onerous and technical to deal with 'in-house' without huge investment in people, time and money.

Key to dealing with the issue of cybercrime is first acknowledging it is a reality and one which will increase in intensity. Next is understanding that unless you properly invest the time and money to deal with the issue in-house, bringing in specialists with technical know-how is the only other serious option.

3. Increased susceptibility of small business IT networks from physical hazards

"It won't happen to me..." is the common refrain from business owners who neglect planning for any contingency. But, like cybercrime, the effect of not planning against the most common physical threats to a business of fire, flood and theft is severe.

It has been widely reported that a large proportion of businesses (up to 80% according to some reports) who are affected by a major incident either never re-open to business or close down within 18 months. Whether the figure really is this high, it's certainly true that not thinking about disaster recovery within your business has the potential to bring it to its knees should a problem hit you.

Your server is often the hub of your business. On it is hosted all your key applications and your customer data, arguably the most important part of your business. When fire tears through an office or a server is ripped from the heart of your business through theft, the ability of a business to continue as if nothing had happened is severely tested.

With these trends in mind, it's time to look towards an alternative to the traditional server-based IT network.

That alternative is cloud computing. While SME's have been slow to see the benefits of the cloud, it's no wonder as we'll soon discover. It's nothing less than a revolution in the way your office operates… but it can seem a daunting step (even though it needn't be).

Before we delve into what cloud technology means and how it works - as well as the benefits over traditional IT approaches - it's worth briefly considering the motivating factors behind businesses currently turning to cloud services.

According to a UK government report on information technology, the main reasons for businesses using cloud services in the UK are:

- Flexibility in meeting business demands

- Quicker disaster recovery

- Automation of software updates

- Increased collaboration between employees

- Reduction of costs

- Predictable cost of using cloud services

As we'll discover in the coming chapters, these are real and tangible benefits that businesses, large and small, can enjoy.

A Cloud primer

What is cloud technology?

Computing has evolved massively in the few decades since the first computer made its way into a modern office.

In those days a single computer was available to the one individual who needed access to a glorified calculator, usually accounts or credit control.

Later came computers in the form of word processors giving secretarial and admin the opportunity to digitise the work being done by typewriters and shorthand. This also allowed dot matrix printing and so the evolution of the computer into the office began.

In those days, physical storage media, such as tapes and disks, were used to transport data between computers. Then came internal networking, as well as mainframe/terminal working, which allowed 'informal' connection of local area networks and individual computers.

Although the 'internet' took it first steps when four computers were successful networked together in the 1969 in a project known as ARPANET, it wasn't until the late 1990s and after the invention of the world wide web, that digital media really started to take over.

Once it was possible to effectively create a network of computers, it was possible to share information in one location. In an office, this would be a computer dedicated to the purpose, called a server. Forgetting the additional services - such as email, web and print services - which would be run on an office server, the emergence of the server as the digital hub of the office become prevalent.

Up to this point a few years ago, the fundamental basis for a company's IT infrastructure was physical. It was rooted in physical hardware, with desktops, printers and other peripherals physically wired to servers kept within the building. This would be wired to a broadband and telephony connection to allow usage of internet and voice services.

As communications providers offered higher speeds of broadband as they upgraded their networks, more and more applications were available to access and share using the internet.

Suddenly, there was a shift in thinking from IT services providers back to mainframes and terminals. Due to improved broadband access and better latency, coupled with lowering costs, delivery of applications and services via the internet became a real possibility.

This was the invention of cloud computing, with cloud loosely meaning 'the internet'. The rise of cloud computing will herald the transformation from physical-based IT networks to internet-based networks, using the shared resources of the internet to provide a more scalable, resilient and secure way of doing everything you were able to do in the office.

Rather than applications sitting locally on your desktop or laptop computer, using local processing power and storage, your most used applications could be accessed remotely and, being hosted online, would offer you better, more reliable performance than your creaking device.

This is the basis of cloud technology: using the internet to deliver all those services available to you in your office, such as back up, servers and applications.

And how does it work?

Imagine your server and everything on it, including all your files, images and financial data as a box. A box of your data.

Now this box represents everything which is physically held on your server sat in the corner of your office (or in your server room).

Like this:

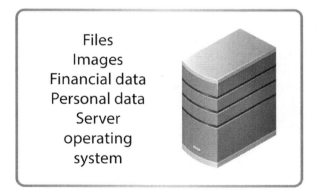

Files
Images
Financial data
Personal data
Server
operating
system

Now picture your own desktop computer, again with the files you keep on it as well as the programmes, such as Word and Excel, and any other 3rd party software.

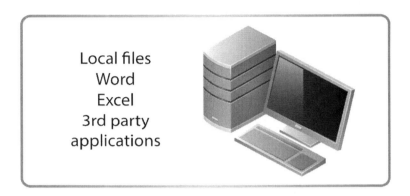

Local files
Word
Excel
3rd party
applications

Picture your desktop computer with a cable running to this box.

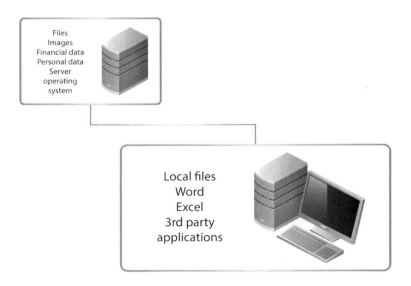

Files
Images
Financial data
Personal data
Server
operating
system

Local files
Word
Excel
3rd party
applications

This is basically your network. When you want to use applications, you access these on your local computer. When you want to access items, either data or an application, that is on the server, you send a 'request' along the cable connecting your computer and server and it calls up the information you need and displays it on your screen.

Now if you want to access the internet, you'll also do this via a cable (which connects to a router connected to a telephone or fibre-optic cable). For the purposes of this demonstration, let's show the internet as a cloud.

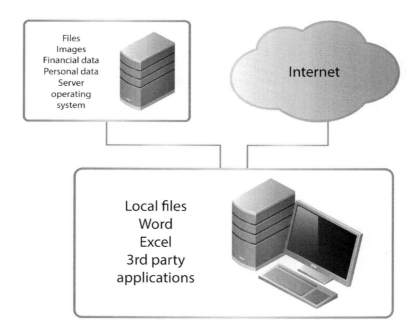

Now imagine another box which, again is a server; but this one is placed within a data centre.

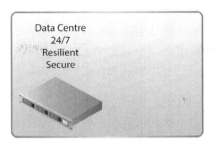

This data centre isn't any old building. It has huge amounts of security, it's overseen 24/7 and has security on the doors. It's also incredible resilient. It has two power supplies flowing into the building as well as multiple network connections; just in case one fails. If the power supplies weren't enough, it even has its own back-up generators so if, in the unlikely event both power supplies fail, it can generate its own power and continue to run.

Now picture a second cable running from your computer but this time just to a cloud (the Internet) and from here the cable runs to the box in data centre.

It would look like this:

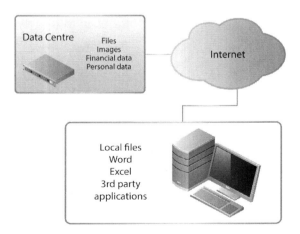

Now imagine if you dragged all the files and data you had on your server onto the server in the data centre. And, then, you dragged all the local files and applications you had on your computer onto the server in the data centre.

So now the data centre has ALL the files and applications on your computer and ALL the files and data stored in your office server. So it looks something like this:

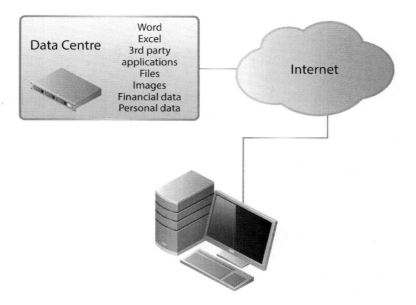

Your office server is empty and your desktop computer is free of files. Now you're able to access all your services and applications in the data centre simply by connecting through the internet. It's now possible to connect through the internet and open a desktop which looks exactly the same. All your services and applications are available as before... but you're connecting to this through the internet rather than a physical cable in the office.

This now means you can access all your applications and your desktop just by connecting through the internet. You can do this anywhere in the world where there is an internet connection and through just about any device. Like this:

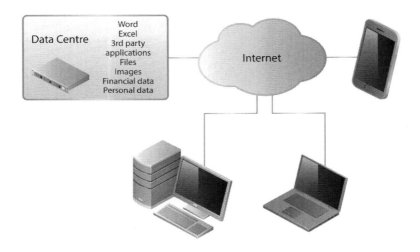

So what's the benefit? Firstly, you no longer need the server in the office as all your services and applications are still available to you via your computer. The difference is they're now hosted off-site in a data centre and are accessible via the internet.

When you look at the screen on your desktop computer, you see your usual desktop, but it's not actually sitting on your computer. What you're looking at is an image of your desktop, which sits in the server in the data centre.

This is key to understanding remote - or hosted - desktop, one of the primary pillars of cloud computing; what you are seeing is only an image of what is on the cloud server.

Therefore, the only thing your computer needs to be able to do in order to access all your services is have a web browser and internet connection.

Without any applications on your desktop or locally stored files, the amount of processing power your computer needs vastly reduces.

And, as for the server, it's no longer doing anything. It can be removed from the office.

This, in the most simplistic terms, is how cloud computing works and demonstrates its power. The availability via the internet of all your applications hosted in a secure data centre means you can access what you need for the office wherever you are. Using the above diagram, all you need to do is connect to the internet via a laptop or another computer and you have full access to your office suite.

If you want to add new users, rather than having to extend the network and provision more hardware and user licences on the server, it's a case of allowing them to connect via the internet.

Cloud business: why now?

Like many technological advances, the development of cloud computing was not consumer-driven. In fact, most consumers hadn't even thought about cloud computing as a solution.

Most of the development of internet-based services was actually derived from the two most popular online industries: pornography and gambling.

The emergence of The Cloud and cloud computing came when two key elements aligned:

- The possibility of being able to use a remote server

- The improved bandwidth to access those servers without any loss of performance

Technology has become much better. Combined with the expansion of broadband and wifi, it has made cloud office services viable. Also, improvements in the quality and bandwidth of broadband services have made remote working much more reliable.

Now we know how cloud computing works and what drove its emergence, the next question is: why?

Why have major corporations and IT services providers been so keen to jump on the cloud computing bandwagon?

What are the advantages of cloud computing?

In discussing what businesses want from technology, we discovered above that a new method of using technology wasn't exactly a pressing need.

As Henry Ford famously said:

"If I had asked people what they wanted, they would have said faster horses"

In the same sense, if you had asked business owners what they wanted from technology, they would most likely have said:

"We just want it to work"

But what has become available is a new, managed solution which provides the best opportunity yet to kill off the technology problems hindering your business once and for all.

Cloud computing helps your business by:

- Putting an end to day-to-day IT problems, such as crashing servers

- Automatically backing-up and protecting your data against malicious attack or breach

- The ability to scale your infrastructure with your operation quickly and easily and without needing to inject huge capital sums

- Allowing staff to work remotely or by allowing outsourced labour to access data securely and in a controlled manner

- Reducing and ultimately controlling the costs of your IT spend so you can properly forecast and plan growth

- Offering in-built disaster recover, since you can access your data and applications from just about any location

In the next section, I'll cover each of these benefits in detail, highlighting the current challenges facing businesses in each area and discussing how cloud computing rises to the challenge. I'll also reveal how you can harness The Cloud to realise these benefits for your business.

Part II
The Cloud
revealed

1

Managing to manage

How to stop firefighting and focus on building your business

There was a time when technology was a byword for saving time.

There was also a loose idea technology could you save you money and, ultimately, improve productivity and effectiveness. Technology would give you a competitive advantage.

What happened?

Unlike consumer technology in the home, including dishwashers and washing machines, which have fulfilled this promise, ask small business owners whether technology actually makes life easier and I'm sure you'll receive a resounding "no".

While the truth of it is technologies such as email and web access have made a huge difference to how small businesses operate and market themselves, on a day-to-day basis, IT problems always *appear* to be present.

Whether it's something as simple as not being able to send an email or not being able to print, technology is blamed as being more hindrance than enabling force.

It can be an emotive issue. When you're on the line and you have an important quote to get to a client by the end of play, the inexplicable reason why you're unable to send an email produces more than frustration. It makes you feel helpless, out of control and as though technology is somehow conspiring against you.

It needn't be this way. Yet corporations big and small put up with a substandard technology infrastructure day-in, day-out because of lack of investment and understanding about what technology can reasonably do.

Of course, the other major problem is providers of technology often require your business to fit in with their product. Unless you have the vast spending power of a corporate to have an IT solution tailored specifically around your particular needs, there is always some element of workaround or adaptation to fit with the technology solution being provided.

The hidden cost of firefighting

Far from the image of the IT department running amok, IT managers often find themselves greatly frustrated by the limitations of technology.

Rather than being able to work on ways to help the business use technology to move forward, speed up processes and grow, they are instead caught in a vicious cycle of firefighting.

Issues caused by lack of user training or insufficient resources regularly overwhelm the IT departments of most major businesses on a day-to-day basis.

If your business has an IT manager, think about this for a second: Does your IT manager spend most of their time responding to and resolving technical issues? What if, instead of dealing with problems, their time was employed finding new ways to work better and smarter?

But, I hear you say, isn't that what an IT person is for? To fix IT problems? Yes. But in a marketplace where overheads are one of the big issues for business, wouldn't it make more sense to use a wage for someone who contributes growth to your business rather than being consumed with technical issues?

Could you imagine what a difference this could make to your organisation? What if you had an individual empowered to drive technology in your business to actually help make sales, service customers, find new business and increase profitability? What if they were tasked with proactively creating projects and rolling out initiatives, rather than patching up issues and reacting to problems?

It may be the person currently responsible in your business for IT development isn't the right type of person… but this is a vision of what IT *should* be doing.

In your business, you may not have a dedicated IT manager. Who is left to deal with situations when they do arise? Is it an administrator or a secretary? Do you know just how much time *they* spend dealing with technology issues? If you're not completely sure, ask them.

Chances are you'll be surprised at how much of their productive time is taken up dealing with technical problems, handling user issues or liaising on IT problems with your external IT support provider. This time could be used far more productively.

Here's the root of the problem: technology issues in your business are costing you money.

Every time an employee's time and focus is taken away from their primary job, it diminishes the ability of the business to work efficiently and effectively.

Every time the business stops working as effectively as it can, something is sacrificed. Either it's the time and effort of other employees, or the quality of the service you provide to your customers or the ability of the business to win new customers. Somewhere, your business is paying for the focus being taken away by technical issues.

And, ultimately, it means your competitors benefit.

So let's sum it up. Constant IT issues cost your business in several ways:

•   Cost of actual repairs and changes

- Time cost of employees suffering from IT problems

- Cost of lack of focus from employees for duration of the IT problem

- Lost opportunity cost of employee for time which cannot be clawed back

- Lost opportunity cost of knowledgeable tech staff spending their time on routine firefighting rather than exploiting technology to the benefit of the business

As you can see, there is only direct monetary cost associated with the cost of repairs in the first bullet (although this shouldn't be underestimated in the case of, for example, a server failure).

The remaining cost to the business is in the commodity we're never able to recover: time. This is the real, hidden cost of technology issues to your business.

A new vision of in-house IT

Cloud computing offers an alternative vision of technology working within your business.

Instead of the IT function being seen as a reactive, problem-focused part of the business, cloud computing hands IT managers a way of transforming their focus to being proactive.

A company's transition to a cloud-based network has an immediate impact on the business and how it works.

No physical server hardware

Cloud technology, in an instant, transforms your office. There is no longer a need for costly items of server hardware taking up valuable office space.

Without a physical server, businesses no longer need to dedicate entire rooms to housing equipment and all the logistical and security issues arising from it.

The only hardware still required within a business are the users' actual desktop or laptop computers, printers and a means of connecting to the internet.

How would your office look without a server taking up valuable space?

With the cost of office floor space at a premium, just think what you may be able to do with the space freed up. Removing servers to make more space for employees or improve the office environment are just some of the benefits of not being tied to physical hardware once a move to a cloud network has been made.

No server failures

The worst possible problem to strike a business is server failure.

The cost of dealing with the consequences of a server which stops working spreads well beyond the (very high) expense of simply replacing the physical hardware.

A server failure not only knocks out a whole business during the time a replacement is being created or a repair is being effected. It brings with it long terms costs associated with lost opportunities and puts the business on the back foot.

In fact, a business which experiences a major server failure and which doesn't have a disaster recovery plan in place is far more likely to go out of business than one which has measures in place. It's *that* serious.

A cloud-based solution immediately eradicates this issue.

Because your IT is hosted remotely on a server in a data centre, server failure isn't critical. The time it takes to bring services back online is much shorter (often seconds) and recovery is possible, which isn't always the case with on-site servers. Cloud services providers set up your solution so that, even in the unlikely event the server in the data centre where your network is hosted does fail, it is rapidly brought back online by switching to another server.

Your server could fail, explode and be smashed into tiny little pieces and, if you were using a cloud-based solution, you might never know. (Although your cloud service provider probably would.)

No unexpected costs

Without the threat of server failure hanging over your head, the cost implications are removed.

The average cost of a server is £5,000-£10,000, including operating system licences and build time, which needs to be found immediately should a problem arise. This, in turn, negatively impacts cash flow.

Then, there's the time cost. In the event of server failure, it would take three days or more to rebuild and restore the server onto new hardware. There's even a good chance that because the hardware is new, you simply won't be able to just 'restore' your applications and data, requiring a rebuild which takes longer.

The main concern with IT support costs is unpredictability.

Once moved onto a cloud computing system, you've effectively outsourced the maintenance and repair of your server to a cloud provider while maintaining complete control.

But this is nothing compared with the savings in cost on software licences.

No costly upgrades and licenses

Do you know how long IT support spends dealing with security upgrades and patches?

With the level of malicious activity so high, in-house IT must regularly cope with the ongoing demands of updating software to ensure it stays free from viruses, malware and attacks which threaten to bring down or disrupt your network.

Failing to stay on top of these updates could be fatal to the business (see Chapter 2).

Nevertheless, the perpetual cycle means time and resource is spent running to simply stand still.

Cloud-based networks handle all the operating system upgrades centrally so not one second of time is spent within your business checking for and implementing upgrades and patches on a daily basis.

Although, you'll still need to protect your local devices, such as desktops and laptops, the consequences of infection are also greatly reduced if all your data is in the cloud.

No doubt, the cost of Microsoft Office licences and upgrades are a cause of consternation when the investment requests are made. But, in many cases, these are unavoidable to ensure software packages and operating systems continue to work with each other, or to take advantage of developments and improvements.

Because of the structure of cloud computing provision, based on monthly licence fees per user, there is provision for using whatever version of packages, such as Microsoft Office, your business needs.

Not every business wants the latest version and so being able to choose when you want to upgrade is in your hands. For example, as a cloud provider we give our customers the ability to run all the currently supported versions, so they're not forced to upgrade to the latest version as soon as it becomes available. Of course, many customers like to stay up to date with the latest version and so the ability to upgrade when these are made available is a great benefit.

The really good cloud services providers include upgrades for no extra charge per month.

In-house IT becomes pro-active...

There is a significant advantage moving to a cloud solution for companies with an existing IT support function.

Moving company IT infrastructure from a physical hardware-based network to a network which relies on no physical infrastructure within an office - except the actual users' desktop computers and laptops and network routers - transforms the function of IT support.

A survey by Microsoft of industrial businesses using cloud technology found their IT functions had been transformed by the move to cloud-based networks. IT departments were taking a more strategic position with 76% of those surveyed saying they were now focused on improving business processes while 71% said quality control was now on the agenda.[4]

... or you get rid of in-house IT support completely

With everything outsourced externally, your business has the opportunity to dispense with in-house IT support completely.

---

[4] 'Cloud computing rains cost savings' 08/04/2011 *Industry Week* http://www.industryweek.com/emerging-technologies/cloud-computing-rains-cost-savings-productivity-benefits

Cloud services effectively takes your IT and transplants it in The Cloud. It then becomes the responsibility of your cloud services provider to support its infrastructure and your everyday needs.

Gaining the competitive advantage

The emergence of cloud computing brings an element alluded to earlier: the ability to leverage technology to help your business grow.

Once you have removed the traditional problems clogging up your business and strangling the time and productivity of your workforce, opportunities arise.

Small businesses, in particular, tend not to understand how cloud technology applies to them. The perception is cloud systems are the exclusive domain of corporations, yet at all levels of business the benefits of cloud computing are being felt.

It's a telling sign of how businesses who have already adopted cloud services now view the transformation.

One survey of business leaders found 55% of users had experienced a competitive advantage through using cloud services. Another 23% said they expected to benefit from a competitive advantage in the future.[5]

Another piece of research found 59% of small and medium-sized companies who had adopted cloud

---

[5] The Cloud Industry Forum, May 2014

technology within their business had reported significant productivity benefits, compared with only 30% of non-cloud users.

There's a clear competitive advantage to be gained by embracing the opportunities cloud computing offers.

2

Protecting your assets

The benefits of secure cloud computing

The most important asset in your business is your data.

The detailed and sensitive data you hold on your customers and your company's systems and financial information are, without doubt, the centre of your business.

Should anything happen to these, the very survival of your business would be in jeopardy.

Figures vary on the subject, but some studies have placed the failure rate of businesses at around 80 to 90% within the two years following a major data loss.

To give a picture of how data loss could affect the ability of your company to function, ask yourself this:

Would you be able to walk into your office tomorrow and carry out your business as normal without any access to the information held on your IT infrastructure?

Most business owners shudder at this possibility. Yet so few plan for what they consider to be once-in-a-lifetime occurrences, including:

- Power failure

- Fire

- Flood

- Theft

- Attacks by hackers

The ability for a company to bounce back from any of these scenarios is a measure of its resilience and the effectiveness of its disaster recovery planning.

For each of these scenarios, let's consider the possible aftermath as the consequences of the data loss increases in severity as you move towards intentional and malicious attacks.

Power failure

How long could your business survive without power? A few hours? What about a few days? And, then, what about broadband? How long could your business function without access to email and the web?

The simple scenario of sustained power loss appears so innocuous on the outside, yet the fact so many businesses fail to plan for this not-too-uncommon problem obviously means the consequences haven't been fully thought-through.

The first stage of any business's disaster recovery plan will begin with what to do in the event of power loss. While most businesses won't be able to extend their contingency budgets to external generators or move towards becoming energy independent, some consideration of how to mitigate sustained power loss should be built in *before* disaster strikes.

Fire/flood

In the UK, at least, the occurrence of natural disasters has been high on the agenda of local government and business. After the widespread flooding in early 2014 in areas previously untouched by rising waters, there is a heightened sense of needing to deal with the consequences of flood damage in business.

It goes without saying water and electronic hardware are very poor bedfellows. The flooding of an office or building housing electronic equipment, such as desktop computers or a server, will certainly render all the inventory unusable.

Similarly, with fire damage. The nature of using electronic equipment in an office and need to maintain a server, usually means there is a greater awareness of the need to ensure electrical wiring is maintained to a high standard. The reason most servers are given a dedicated room is the need to also install cooling such as fans or air conditioning to mitigate the heat from their constant usage. Again, in itself this creates a greater fire risk.

Fire risk is considered more fully than other forms of risk, due to company health and safety obligations requiring regular fire hazard checks.

Theft

While the immediate aftermath of theft within a business is almost exactly the same as dealing with the fire damage and flooding, the long-term consequences are potentially far more damaging.

Fire and flooding result in data loss. The data is lost, but the consequences end there. With theft, there is an additional element of malice and intent.

The direct purpose of the act of theft may be to take valuable electronic equipment or money from the office. However, the loss of the information to the individuals responsible for the crime puts your business in a much more difficult situation: you now have no control over the data which has been compromised.

If data held on desktop computers, hard drives, external media and on the server itself is taken, there are multiple ways the information could be used for malicious purposes. These range from using personal and confidential details of customers to transact banking fraud to industrial espionage.

The effects of this element of data loss can be huge.

Estimates of the cost of reputational damage for SMEs was between £1,500 and £8,000 and £25,000 to £115,000 for larger businesses. The breaches which attracted the most media attention were for system failure, data loss and breaches of confidentiality.[6]

---

[6] Cyber Security Technical Report 2013 PwC

Few businesses would like to be in the position of having to tell their loyal customers, "we're sorry, but we've lost your personal and financial data and we have no idea who has it or what they're going to do with it…".

Attacks by hackers

Again, there is a subtle but important difference between the danger posed by theft and attacks from hackers. While an office theft may disrupt a business and cause huge data loss, there is always the possibility the individuals responsible for the physical theft only have their sights on the immediate proceeds of crime. In other words, the sale of the physical equipment stolen or acquisition of money or items of value. There is a chance the subsequent data loss is a by-product of the original crime.

In the case of attacks by hackers, however, there is no doubt as to intent: it is to steal or disrupt data.

What is clear is attacks like these now represent the biggest threat to small and medium sized businesses in the UK, partly through a lack of understanding their network is vulnerable.

The National Crime Agency (NCA) in the UK early in 2014 warned of several areas where cyber criminals were a threat to UK businesses over the next three years.[7] These included compromising company networks to steal data to gain a competitive advantage, damage user confidence,

---

[7] 'National Crime Agency lists cyber criminals as major UK threat' 02/05/2014 *ITPro* http://www.itpro.co.uk/security/22177/national-crime-agency-lists-cyber-criminals-as-major-uk-threat

control infrastructure or inflict reputational damage and targeted disruption of networks.

It also pointed to a continued threat from large scale harvesting of business data specifically to commit fraud using malware or mobile technology.

Worryingly, the NCA identifies small business as the soft underbelly for cyber criminals who are focused on hitting companies with "less mature security measures".

This isn't to say businesses are burying their heads in the sand about the threat from attacks on their networks.

In fact, a global survey by Ernst & Young put the UK ahead of other countries as recognising cybercrime as a major threat to their organisations with 74% of businesses in the UK classing it as high risk, compared with 49% globally.[8]

However, 36% of businesses said they were more concerned with the cyber threat from their own employees compared with 26% who considered organised crime more of a threat.

Is this a case of the enemy within? No. What this reflects is an understanding by business that it is usually employees who are the 'weak link' in the information security chain. Threats from employees opening spurious emails, leaking passwords, illicitly transferring files or downloading viruses onto the network can all be a prelude to the execution of more serious crimes.

---

[8] EY 13th Global Fraud Survey 11/06/2014

The extent of threats to a business from natural disaster, accidental damage and more malicious forms of attack rarely hit home until it actually happens.

Prevention is always the best - and most cost-effective - method of ensuring your business continues to run smoothly and data loss does not occur. It requires forward planning and developing measures such as information security policies to educate employees and adhere to standards, as well as technical solutions to mitigate against data loss.

DOWNLOAD - Discover how to develop an information security policy for your business.

Go to www.worknet.co.uk/infosecurity to download a free step-by-step guide to developing your own information security policy to help you and your staff minimise the chance of malicious attacks.

Knowing the extent of the threat, consider how most SMEs in the UK protect their most valuable asset.

Backing-up to tape

The traditional means to protect against potential data loss is through the process of regularly back-ups, with back-up to tape still the most common method for servers. If a server is knocked out of action through fire or water damage, the business is protected and can be back on its feet using the latest set of back-ups, with only minimal data loss.

Your businesses may still be backing up to disk or tape. At set regular intervals, you will manually insert a blank or rewritable disk or tape and copy over the essential data for running your business. In many cases, this won't be all your data - possibly just the key financial and accounts data.

The problem with this situation is it relies on two elements to be effective:

• Regularly and consistently undertaking the back-ups

• Storage of the media in a secure and protected environment

The importance of the first point is self-evident. Without undertaking the process regularly - at the very least, daily - there is little point in making back-ups. Information moves so quickly and the situation changes that out-of-date information is often just as useless as no data.

However, in terms of storage of media this is where many businesses fall down.

I've personally visited businesses who have religiously backed-up their data only to compromise its security by leaving the back-up media on a shelf above the server itself or in the drawer of a desk.

The separation and distance of data from its source is the main benefit of back-up. If something happens in the office to compromise the server and your data - such as a fire or theft - it makes little sense if your back-up data is in the same location and left unprotected.

I would even argue, this is *more* dangerous. In the case of theft, it is much, much easier for a thief to lift a handful of disks than tear an entire server from its rack.

The lasse-faire approach of some businesses to the storage of back-up media is, at best, wholly pointless and, at worst, making it even easier for data loss to occur.

Backing-up to an external hard drive

As optical storage media have diminished in importance and popularity, many businesses have turned to external hard drives as a way of storing back-up data.

There are many benefits, including being able to store greater content on a hard drive, improved resilience and less chance of a disk being scratched or broken and being rendered unusable. An external hard drive is a lot easier to handle than a set of optical disks, but more difficult to archive long term.

However, the benefits of an external hard drive are quickly outweighed by the disadvantages depending on how it is being stored once data is backed-up.

The ideal situation is to store the hard drive in a safe or other secure, water-tight, fire-proof area.

The least ideal situation is - as with optical disks or tapes - leaving the hard drive in the office or, even worse, removing it to a less secure environment. I've heard numerous stories about people leaving the office with the hard drive in their backpack or bag, believing this to be the safest way of protecting data.

Just like losing a laptop, the instant your data goes out the door your actions can pose a greater risk to your company and your customers than any other action.

Furthermore, back-ups are only as good as your ability to restore from the back-up. Most businesses never test their ability to recover data from back-up unless there has been a failure. By that time, if you discover you are unable to recover from your back-up media, it's too late.

Using an online back-up service

Many companies using an IT support company will be familiar with online back-up services. This may be the first interaction they've had with a cloud-based service.

Instead of burning your data onto a disk or hard drive periodically, you're effectively burning your data onto a space on a server off-site. Furthermore, it will most likely be set to automatically back-up at a certain time each day to avoid having to process it manually.

This solution removes the problematic elements of the first two options. Your back-ups are being made off-site and there is no manual interference - so it will be done.

It doesn't come without its issues, however. Automatic back-ups are usually dependent on factors such as certain computers being left on during the back-up period or the server remaining on and available for the duration. If this doesn't happen the back-up doesn't happen.

There are also wild variations in the quality of the back-up services available. If something goes wrong, how easy is it to retrieve your data as quickly as possible? US-based solutions which require a call to an international customer service centre may not prove the most effective.

Similarly, the use of US-based companies brings up the question of how safe your data really is. For more on this subject turn to page 104 for a discussion of the implications of the USA Patriot Act.

How hosting on the cloud differs from an in-house system

The problems of IT security and lack of resilience in in-house systems are well-known. It's why finally being free of these deep-seated problems has been a revelation for businesses making the jump to cloud-based networks.

According to a Microsoft survey, 94% of business who have switched to cloud computing reported an improvement in security, while 75% said network availability had improved.

There are four key benefits in terms of security and resilience that cloud computing delivers:

Resilience

Adopting cloud services on which to base your IT gives your business much-needed resilience. Running an in-house server leaves your business exposed to any of the problems outlined above; in these cases your business's resilience in low.

By hosting your IT off-site in a secure data centre, your resilience is immediately improved. Regardless of what happens to your office or physical premises, your ability to bounce back from disaster is very high; all your data and applications are safely and securely hosted.

When you are hit with a disaster and your server is damaged, the amount of time it takes you to get the business back on its feet is numbered in days and weeks.

When your IT is hosted in The Cloud, your ability to keep your business running is measured in minutes and hours.

Because your access point to your own IT is via the internet, you can simply use a laptop or other device with an internet connection and carry on working as if nothing had happened.

You could walk into your office to find a disaster had occurred and within minutes have informed your staff to remain at home using their home PCs or laptops to access the company's IT. Or you could continue working in the office using laptops as long as there was an internet connection available.

Aberdeen Group research found businesses using cloud services were able to resolve issues in an average of 2.1 hours, a significant difference from businesses which didn't use cloud services with an average resolution time of 8 hours. Equate this to more than one working day to resolve the issue and you can see the impact it could have on your business.

A disaster really doesn't have to break your business's stride. Cloud computing helps you maintain business efficacy.

Constant, reliable back-up

Relying on manual back-ups onto disks or hard drives, or using a low-cost back-up service within the office all bring their own problems.

Hosting your IT in The Cloud means your back-ups can be taken directly and automatically at source. There is no danger of failed back-ups because machines were not available, nor missed back-ups because of human error.

Good cloud providers will ensure your entire data is backed-up periodically; should the highly unlikely problem occur of a hosted server you're using being damaged, the back-up image of your data can quickly be restored.

No fiddling with back-up tapes, no struggling to find the latest back-up and no spending hours waiting on an international customer service telephone line trying to locate your back-up. And no tearing out your hair working out how to restore your data and your databases.

Hosting in the cloud offers unprecedented levels of reliability and, taking the human element out of the equation, gives you peace of mind your whole network is protected.

Controlled access

As highlighted in survey after survey, one of the main threats to the security of your IT is your own employees.

Whether by accident or with malicious intent, anyone who has access to your IT has the power to do damage. The problem of a physical network, spread through an office of desktop computers are the number of entry points through which viruses, malware and other issues which can cause disruption. Of course, your 'network' still exists, but the effect of the malware is significantly reduced as there is no server.

With hosted cloud services, those gaps don't exist. There is only one entry point to the network in and out through the remote desktop log-in.

Because it is a controlled environment - and all the necessary applications and files are hosted remotely - as a business owner or IT manager you have complete control over access.

For example, it is possible to prevent users from accessing certain email programmes well known for their problems with spam or social media sites, such as Facebook and Twitter. You can literally lock the system down.

You can also monitor activity in terms of what users have accessed. If the need arises to trace activity of a particular user, this can be done.

The access rights can also be revoked and amended within minutes should this be necessary. The damage wreaked by a disgruntled employee or information compromised by a worker going off to a competitor can seriously impact your business. Cloud services give businesses the overarching control through which they can manage those who use the network.

Managed

Security is cited as being one of main concerns for businesses with regards their IT infrastructure.

Some businesses - such as those holding confidential customer data - are more wary of the consequences of a security breach and have built systems to ensure their data remains secure.

Having invested time and money in those systems, it is understandable why there is a reluctance to suddenly uproot everything they've done to move to a fully managed cloud-based network.

This factor is one of the biggest obstacles for wider adoption of cloud computing technology among businesses. But being wedded to systems which aren't necessarily perfect, but at least 'do the job' is both a drawback and an advantage, depending on which side of the fence you sit.

If you have these systems in your business, it feels like there is more than a technical upheaval involved in transplanting your systems to The Cloud. There is an emotional element around letting go and handing control over your network to an unknown quantity. It's the job of cloud providers (such as my company, Worknet) to demonstrate we can be trusted to manage your IT.

If you're a business without those systems in place, there's an opportunity for you to skip all the growing and development pains associated with trying to pull a solution together and go straight for the prize.

By far the biggest advantage of a managed approach is allowing you to stop having to think about IT at an infrastructure level.

Your IT is just there… working for you.

Not having to pay attention to the infrastructure issues on a day-to-day basis frees your time to think about how you can use IT and technology to move your business forward. Resources, time and effort can be dedicated to doing valuable profit-building work, such as finding more customers, improving service levels and enhancing productivity.

3

Growing through technology

How cloud technology gives your business scale and flexibility

We all have plans in business. We know exactly where we want to be and put the measures in place to try and arrive at our desired end point.

But predicting how your business is going to look in three months' time, let alone one year or five years, is often impossible.

The experience of the last recession caught many businesses unaware and those who had invested in expansion and taking on staff found themselves struggling to adapt to the new landscape of austerity.

Similarly, as we're moving out of recession, the sudden burst of growth has made it tough on businesses burned by their pre-recession experience from moving too fast.

This cautious approach isn't good for business... but who can blame them?

It's why such an emphasis is placed on planning. The reality is planning for the needs of your business in three, six or 12 months is really, at best, guesswork.

From a traditional IT infrastructure perspective, guessing the needs of future growth has been the only method businesses could work to.

If you were planning to make a major investment in upgrading your IT and server capabilities, you had better be sure you had factored in the additional capacity needed in the next 18 months at least and probably for at least three years.

If you didn't factor in future growth or if you made an error with these figures, you could find yourself paying for a major upgrade even sooner than you thought.

Worse, you may not have the ability to grow as you need. The advantage cloud technology brings in allowing people to work flexibly from different locations means you don't need to worry so much about planning office space. It is entirely possible to take advantage of disparate locations (often at an opportunistic price) and get people working together.

Equally, having to factor in future growth is good when the growth materialises. When the business doesn't grow as expected, you're left with a network being under-utilised while capital has been unnecessarily tied up in a project which hasn't reaped the extent of its benefits yet.

This is wasted investment. And it can have an impact on day-to-day issues, such as cash flow.

The 'problem' of growth

When you build a server, you need to know how many users it is going to support. It is ill-advised to knowingly install a server which will only support 10 users when your business is projected to have 20 users within the next 12 months. Your IT needs to support your growth.

But, as a business, what do you do?

You have two choices:

• Pay upfront for the possibility of growth by investing in a bigger server with the capacity to add more users in the hope you'll grow, or

• Upgrade to your existing level (for lower cost) and risk the possibility of double investment if you need to replace or upgrade the server within the next 24 months.

Either of these are a risk and it requires you, as a business, to make a judgment call which is almost unknowable.

For most businesses who have growth as an aim, defining the extent of their immediate growth and their needs in terms of labour and infrastructure is guesswork. In many ways, you have to place an arbitrary point on a cost Vs future capability curve.

Very few businesses and business owners feel they're able to do that. Fortunately, the new model of cloud computing allows both flexibility and scalability in your business whether it is for growth or contraction.

The Cloud: a new model of flexibility

Cloud services operate on a completely different model from traditional IT infrastructure.

Instead of the major, upfront cost of building the network from the server outwards, the better cloud computing services operate on a 'per user' subscription basis.

For example, if your business has ten members of staff, you need only pay for ten users on a fixed cost monthly basis. This will provide access to your hosted cloud network.

From this you can bolt-on additional services through per user licences.

Do all of the users need Microsoft Office? This functionality can be added quickly and easily for an additional fixed monthly fee.

But here's the real benefit. Should a user no longer need Microsoft Office, they can be downgraded and no longer continue to pay the monthly fee.

Minimum contract periods and notice periods may apply depending on the cloud services provider being used, but it offers an entirely new form of flexibility where services are only paid for when being used.

With the monthly 'per user' subscription model, businesses no longer need to toil over calculations around growth and what their future capabilities will need to be.

No longer will they be required to make huge payments in advance of receiving the benefit.

Businesses can quickly and easily start benefiting from a hosted cloud service without the need for major investment and in the knowledge they can upgrade or downgrade their service according to their business and financial needs.

For many businesses the flexibility offered by the cloud computing model to their business is the key driver behind its adoption.

One research paper found 71% of companies surveyed said operational flexibility was their primary reason for shifting to cloud services (the second most important driver was cost savings).[9]

---

[9] 2012 Microsoft/Edge Strategies SMB Cloud Adoption Study

4

The Remote Working Revolution

How cloud computing is setting businesses free

Imagine being able to sit on the beach, open your laptop and have your whole desktop available to you as if you were in the office.

Imagine being in the middle of a client meeting and instantly being able to call up any and every piece of information your company has related to them or the business as if you were in the office.

Imagine being able to keep working on that urgent project without having to pull hours and hours in the office because that's where all the information you need is stored.

With just a laptop and a decent internet connection, all of these things are now a possibility.

And it's all thanks to the power of cloud computing.

Over the last few years, there has been a fundamental shift in the way we work.

No longer do companies feel they need to constrain their employees in the confines of working between the four walls of the office.

No longer do business owners and entrepreneurs immediately see the need to buy office space as soon as they expand their business.

Working remotely - outside the office with just a laptop, at home on a desktop or even from an internet cafe or client office - is not only a reality. It's an opportunity.

Why has remote working become popular?

There are several factors which have helped push the move to remote working:

1) **Cost of space**. Commercial rents and office space has never been more expensive in the UK. Now startups and businesses having finally pulled through the recession are more aware than ever of the benefit of staying agile and lean. This usually means being able to immediately reduce or remove overheads when needed. And rent, along with staff, is one of the biggest. It used to be the case that company expansion meant increasing your office footprint. This need no longer be the case. Adding staff members to increase capability who work predominantly from home or even in another city or country has finally become a normal practice, offering

companies a huge opportunity. However, there are some serious implications in terms of security and productivity, some of which will be dealt with below.

2) **New outsourcing models**. Technology has, to a great extent, facilitated the new and varied models of online outsourcing, but the rise of the outsourcing is not simply a technological phenomenon. Small businesses have long been wishing to tap global resources in terms of technical expertise, creative and design to take advantage of the considerable cost savings which are crucial when building a business. The ability to use a designer in Bangalore or Manila who is working to a higher standard than many of the individuals they may be able to employ in London or Cardiff <u>and</u> at a fraction of the cost and without the need for a long-term contract or time commitment gives them power. It isn't just SME businesses. Major companies have long been advocates of outsourcing overseas with the generational shift of manufacturing and telesales support to the Indian sub-continent and Asia, generally. Again, as most of the big companies have found there are some serious implications of outsourcing which need to be dealt with and appropriate systems put in place. Failing to deal with these means running into the sort of problems companies like HSBC did when their customers' security information was compromised.[10]

3) **Flexible working practices**. The nature of the workplace has changed dramatically over the last 10 years. Finding and recruiting staff is an expensive and

---

[10] 'India data breach hits HSBC' 28/06/06 computing.co.uk http://www.computing.co.uk/ctg/news/1843338/indian-breach-hits-hsbc

time-consuming business. Companies understand it is cheaper and more cost-effective to lower staff attrition by keeping existing staff happier and more content in their jobs; on the flip side they also recognise the need to attract good recruits by offering better perks and incentives. To this end, the increase in the scope and usage of flexible working practices has given workers who struggle with the commute or the once-restrictive 9 to 5 routine a chance to continue within a company. This has been good news for parents, generally, who operate to a different schedule in terms of their children's schooling and often have to leave work at a moment's notice. It has provided opportunities to businesses looking to employ individuals who wouldn't normally fit within the usual recruitment practices. It has also allowed businesses to continue to operate when inclement weather or external circumstances has shut down the office or prevented the majority of the workforce from making it into work. (And an end – perhaps sadly - to the celebratory jump for joy when you open the curtains and see snow in the morning...) For once, working from home isn't a byword for shirking from a hard day's work. It is, for many, an accepted practice which is part of the weekly work mix. Even though flexible working practices are only now being heavily promoted by the UK government, many larger businesses have, out of necessity, had to operate remote working on some level. However, this was usually on the senior executive end of the scale and the need to be able to continue to work even when abroad - for business or pleasure. Senior individuals within a business whose sign-off comes at the end of the approval process are often required to be available 24/7/365 in a fast-moving business. Their availability therefore has become more important than ever. The challenge for the business owner or management of the business in the rise of flexible working has mainly been one in terms of productivity.

These are just three of the factors which have helped grease the wheel of remote working. Other minor factors include new methods of facilitating global payments, improved communication and shifting social attitudes, all of which have contributed in part to this new way of working.

Some industry sectors have been more affected by the remote working revolution than others. Businesses which rely on staff being 'on-the-road' and working on client sites have traditionally struggled with finding technology solutions to suit their model; now, fortunately, the situation is flipped with businesses traditionally seen as office-based trying to find new ways to use the remote working model.

Who is remote working technology helping <u>right now</u>?

There are some business functions where remote working, facilitated by cloud technology, is making a serious commercial impact in both improving customer service, driving sales and increasing productivity in achieving both those goals. And there are some industries where the opportunities offered by remote working could revolutionise every part of their business should they decide to adopt it.

Here are just some of the business areas where remote working through cloud technology is making an impact:

Sales teams

The life of the sales rep is well-documented. Travelling the length and breadth of the country in their luxury car, logging the miles and spending time hopping from one prospect or client to the next. In some businesses, this has an international flavour with sales execs jetting off to far-flung locations to do business and report back to HQ.

For sales teams, cloud computing has allowed unprecedented levels of collaboration between team members. Sales reps have access to information about other reps' activities in real time, thereby pooling available company intelligence and allowing for sharing of opportunities as well as reducing duplication of effort and maximising productivity.

Information management becomes easier with centrally, cloud-based systems through which all relevant information flows into and out from ensuring accuracy and integrity of data being fed to and from sales team members. This gives unprecedented control to sales team leaders and sales directors operating over huge territories who are fed with real time information from any sales rep capable of connecting to the internet.

With sensitive company information held on secure, cloud servers the risks of data loss and security breaches are minimised - compared to the gaping hole of security that carrying a laptop filled with locally stored data used to represent. Furthermore, if situations arise where potential security breaches are flagged up - such as a stolen password or a disgruntled member of staff is threatening to sabotage the system or pull off sensitive data - it takes seconds to shut down access and eliminate the threat.

For sales teams and sales team leaders, the advent of cloud technology has both expanded the power of their teams while, at the same time, giving control to a level previously thought impossible.

Creative and development teams

Design and development are the lynchpin of many organisations. However, for global companies the bringing together of its leading designers, product developers and project managers required vast amounts of time and effort moving bodies across continents and scheduling.

Cloud computing's remote working possibilities have opened up the global collaborative experience to bring in design and creative teams to not only contribute to projects, but to work in real time.

The old maxim used to be 'you need bodies in a room to make something happen' and to some extent it was right. There is, often, little to replace the face-to-face, one-on-one interaction between team members in driving creativity and exploring new ideas.

However, this situation has changed dramatically. Creative teams needn't reside in the same building, or even the same country or continent. In an instant, it is possible to draw together disparate individuals from around the world to collaborate and work on projects. Video networking, chat and real-time collaborative solutions mean you can see, talk with and work on projects together in a way which is only one small step away from being in a room together.

Driven partly by better communication technology and partly by an improvement in the quality of broadband and wifi connectivity globally, these ways of creative working have transformed how businesses from the multinational corporate to the solopreneur working out of his bedroom interact and create with designers and developers to produce the next generation of products and services.

Project management

Project managers rely on the two-pronged arm of control and accountability to hit objectives on time and on budget. Working with teams across geographical boundaries places incredible strain on the ability to keep a grip on costs and maintain a stream of accountability and progress towards key milestones in a project.

The development of cloud-based remote working has given project managers the most powerful tool in their armoury. Instant access and real-time reporting on activities as they are undertaken and completed, regardless of location, and a 360 degree view of the project delivers real benefits to businesses relying on these teams to drive commercial projects.

Velocity and agility are the new watch words of the global economy and any business able to create and implement a product, service or model in the quickest time to reach market or roll out within a business has a distinct advantage. The benefits of cloud remote working gives project teams the opportunity to work from anywhere, anytime and without constraint. Even with projects which require numerous sign-offs and a convoluted approval process, cloud-based remote options allow for instantaneous review and approval or review and amends to shorten the traditional approval cycles to minutes rather than days.

Working on client sites is better facilitated by cloud technology. Those embedded in client companies or regularly working on-site have the ability to retain links with the office and keep both their, and their client's, access secure.

Executive decision-making

It may seem a minor point, but the power of remote working technology to simply connect board room and C-level executives quickly and easily is having a major impact on business.

No longer would the disappearance of a board member for a few weeks likely be a block on major or emergency decision-making. As long as they simply have an internet connection in whatever location they're in, secure access to company documentation in a controlled environment through a cloud-based service delivers both the information they need to make, approve or reject changes.

Without wanting to reinforce a stereotype, this could mean decisions being made whether the exec is residing at home, on the beach or even on a boat crossing the Atlantic. Distance and remoteness has never been less important with the advent of cloud technology.

In each of the functions, there are benefits to be derived from adopting cloud computing technology as a way of facilitating remote working. Those companies which have done this are seeing benefits, already.

With benefits, of course, come challenges. It's not plain sailing in the world of remote working, particularly for businesses who operate distance working policies but are still reliant on the traditional IT model.

Already, our discussion has touched on security and the huge problems around keeping data from falling into the hands of those who would seek to do our business and our customers harm. Fortunately, cloud technology provides the answer to every one of the challenges thrown up by remote working systems.

Challenges for remote working... and how cloud technology overcomes them

There are a number of key concerns for a business with staff working either away from the office or travelling around on a regular basis. Fortunately, the advent of cloud computing technology helps eliminate each of these concerns:

Lost and stolen laptops

It's every business's nightmare (and it's a problem which has affected the government on more than one occasion): a laptop left on a train or in an office filled with sensitive company information and documentation.

The statistics are astonishing. One US study reported around 10,000 laptops are reported lost at 36 US airports every week.

While measures can be put in place to ensure files are encrypted and password protected, the reality is no measure of encryption is safe from a determined and relatively lightly-skilled hacker. Even information you believe you had deleted from the hard drive is accessible by someone who knows what they are doing.

And it's best to assume this is so. Should an errant laptop fall into the hands of a criminal gang, their ability to mine the contents of the machine and use it for all manner of nefarious purposes shouldn't fail to frighten any business for which this could be a potential reality.

Yet, businesses seem hesitant to act and like most IT issues, won't do anything about it until something goes wrong. Potentially, of course, loss of sensitive customer data represents one of the most damaging elements of data loss and the subsequent damage it causes to your reputation. Few businesses recover from this.

Utilising cloud-based technology offers a relatively affordable and almost completely secure method of preventing this from ever happening.

Instead of storing sensitive customer data on the laptop itself, using a hosted desktop or other remote cloud system, the data is stored on a server in the cloud. As the user is required to log into the cloud-based system in order to access whatever information is needed, nothing is stored locally and so a missing laptop does not contain anything likely to cause data loss issues.

There is nothing to hack or force access to, as the data is hosted in the cloud.

It's akin to locking the safe when the loss of the laptop has been reported.

The same applies to using remote computers, such as in business centres or at an internet cafe. Because your desktop is accessible only after log-in, there is no data stored locally and no risk of data loss.

Stolen passwords and log-in

As outlined above, once alerted of any data breach it is possible to immediately shut-out any attempted log-in with passwords and usernames.

The nature of cloud computing allows central control of user access rights. When a user needs to be knocked off the system, immediately, this can be done quickly and simply. Likewise, if a username and password is reported stolen or compromised, user log-in details can be immediately changed.

A good information security policy will, of course, mitigate the issue of password theft with regular changes to passwords made mandatory.

DOWNLOAD - Discover how to develop an information security policy for your business.

Go to www.worknet.co.uk/infosecurity to download a free step-by-step guide to developing your own information security policy to help you and your staff minimise the chance of malicious attacks.

Disgruntled workers and sabotage

Dealing with disgruntled staff is easy in an office. They are simply escorted from the premises and their access from IT systems is immediately revoked - presuming you have someone who can implement this quickly and efficiently.

How do you deal with a disgruntled worker who doesn't operate from your office or who has remote access?

Just think of the damage they could do: access your servers with your customer lists, details and potentially highly valuable information your competitors would love to clap their eyes on, sabotage systems and cause reputational damage by continuing to contact customers and stakeholders. It's like a virtual bull in a china shop.

Fortunately, managed cloud computing solutions offer the benefits of remote working with the security of total control over how a worker access your network.

Firstly, access can be given and revoked almost immediately. The advantage of a cloud-based service is being able limit access instantly; the user accesses their desktop remotely so there is no need to 'block' anything on the laptop or computer they are using.

Secondly, in taking on remote workers you're able to control the level of access they enjoy with a click of a button. Like a traditional office network, certain users don't need to see accounting information while some don't need access to the full customer database. But, unlike the traditional office system, access is more easily granted and revoked when needed.

Furthermore, you don't have to touch any of this. Using a managed approach you're able to maintain full control over access without any of the technical issues.

Thanks to cloud computing, the challenges of remote working no longer outweigh the benefits. The worry lines are finally dissipating on the foreheads of companies' Information Security officers resulting from the loss of control over their IT that remote working practices have caused.

Workable business practice - and a practice which suits employers and employees in equal measure - is being facilitated by cloud technology eradicating the drawbacks.

There has been some debate over the effectiveness and desirability of remote working over the last few years.

While not quite a backlash, many companies have wondered whether all the security risks and potential reductions in productivity are really worth it. Fortunately, cloud computing technology has shown it is possible and it is secure.

Is the tide starting to turn? Maybe, maybe not, but incoming Yahoo chief Marissa Mayer ordered an end of remote working provoking arguments on both sides of the fence.[11]

One thing is certain; remote working is here to stay. And cloud computing is making it a reality for businesses of every size.

---

[11] 'Yahoo chief bans working from home' 25/02/2013 *The Guardian* http://www.theguardian.com/technology/2013/feb/25/yahoo-chief-bans-working-home

5

Controlling Costs

How fixed cost computing is a finance director's best friend

There's an elephant in the room: the impact of cost-savings through adopting cloud services.

Survey after survey show cost-savings are one of the key reasons why businesses turn to cloud-based services in the first instance.

The main areas where cost-savings are achieved are:

- **Reduction in internal IT support costs,** including staff. With a fully managed cloud solution, all support can be dealt with by the cloud service provider.

- **Reduction in software and licensing costs**. Instead of the vast expenditure on purchasing fully owned application and software packages, businesses using cloud services 'pay-as-you-go'. The ability of staff to have access to all the applications they need when they need them and for as long as they need them without the huge cost is a major saving. There is additional value in having access to the latest versions, too, without always having to pay for new licences. It's also beneficial to have everyone in the office working from the same version of an application for reasons of compatibility. (I've been to offices where people are using Microsoft Office 2003, 2007, 2010 and 2013 – all at the same time).

Other data has shown businesses who have enjoyed significant cost savings through cloud computing efficiencies have been able to reinvest this money in activities which help grow the business.

The benefit for forecasting

As discussed in the chapter on scalability and flexibility, predicting the size and nature of your business in a few months, let alone in a few years, is difficult.

Add on top of this the uncertainty inherent with in-house IT infrastructure where problems frequently appear with unforeseen consequences, both in terms of time and budget.

Against this background, being able to accurately and realistically forecast your budgetary needs for the coming year is like pinning a tail on the donkey, blindfolded.

The cloud computing subscription model, on the other hand, provides an antidote to this.

It is now reasonably easy to forecast IT costs - or a narrow parameter of costs - which are likely to be incurred during any period. The fixed price, per user menu of services hands power back to the business owner, or person who holds the purse strings.

Rather than being given an emergency budget for effecting repairs should your server break down or other IT problems needs immediate rectification, finance directors and business owners can plan exactly what they'll need to service their team with the knowledge all IT costs have been capped at what they are paying.

The combination of a fully managed cloud solution, hosted off-site, and its flexible pricing structure gives businesses the power to define costs, look to the future and focus on growth without the constant worry of possibly needing to find budget for unexpected and unplanned in-house IT issues.

Part III
The Cloud for your business

Choosing the right cloud computing provider

How to formulate a strategy to move your business to the cloud

To realise the benefits of moving to the cloud, you need a strategy.

The major obstacle to migrating to cloud computing technology for most businesses is a lack of understanding about how to physically make the change.

This is a problem if this is <u>your</u> business.

If your business puts off migrating to the cloud as soon as possible, you miss out. You miss out on the cost savings. You miss out on the time saved from not having to deal with continuing, time-sapping technology issues. You miss out on the opportunity to gain a competitive advantage in your market. In every way.

There is also perception that a jump to cloud technology can be a serious upheaval. While moving from an office-based server network to a hosted (cloud) network isn't *technically* difficult, the real issues arise from not considering the impact it will have on your day-to-day working practices.

A business making a successful migration to the cloud (or hosted solution) does so after clearly defining their technology needs and planning this in advance of the move. Like any major infrastructure work or upgrade, the more thought that goes into the planning stage the better the result.

Ignore this stage and while the move to the cloud will theoretically get your business operating in a cloud-based environment, there will likely be unintended negative consequences in terms of productivity and the way your business works.

As you'll discover, if you're thinking of moving to the cloud, it is worth considering just how much flexibility and control over your systems you would like to retain as well as how you are likely to use it.

In other words, do you want a system which will fit into the way you work or are you able to make your systems work with a particular fixed cloud solution? This is the crux of what differentiates one cloud provider from another.

And it's usually the explanation of why costs vary so much. A bespoke hosted set-up and management require marginally more investment but ultimately deliver exactly what you need with little upheaval of your current business systems.

In the next chapter, I have provided a comprehensive checklist you can use to assess your business's needs before making a decision about the solution you may need (see page 107)

Once you have fully assessed your business needs, the issue turns to your preferred solution. In considering this, there are some baseline questions:

- Will your business benefit from a specific third party application with a very defined purpose?

- Will your business require a combination of cloud applications?

- Or would your business benefit from moving to a fully hosted and managed cloud solution?

Let's explore each of these areas to discover which cloud-based options are available to your business:

Purpose-specific cloud-based applications

Even if your business is not fully migrated to a cloud solution, it's likely you've experienced the power of cloud technology through one or more applications which have become commonplace in everyday life.

This category comprises some of the better-known cloud applications, including the likes of Dropbox, Skype and Xero. These are applications designed to fulfil a specific purpose. For more individuals and businesses, their interaction with cloud-based technology is usually through these applications which focus on meeting a specific need (and most users wouldn't even think of them in terms of cloud applications).

This may be bookkeeping and accounting, through packages like Kashflow or Xero, project management through Trello or Basecamp, time management through any number of To-do list applications, diary management or storage such as Dropbox and Apple's own iCloud storage solution.

Businesses will likely use two or three cloud-based applications, some of which are compatible with each other and some of which aren't. They will fulfil a particular need and so this element of their work will use a cloud-based application.

Whether this really marks a business as having migrated to the cloud is questionable. Often these applications are used as valuable add-ons to existing infrastructure and data storage in the office.

Dropbox, for example, may be used for backup or document collaboration... but rarely will a business move all of their data to Dropbox instead of holding files locally.

While a business may be using *some* cloud features, it has not fully embraced the range of benefits of cloud; it is simply accessing services which are made available through cloud technology – and often because they aren't available any other way.

Undoubtedly, these applications help speed up the way you work, make your job easier or change how you work for the better. For most people, using these applications is their first taste of the benefits cloud technology can bring to their working life and their business.

But these don't go anywhere near to tapping into the huge benefits, including building greater resilience into your systems, offering flexibility in how your staff work and providing iron-clad security within which your company's and your customers' data can be stored.

Sector-specific cloud-based applications

In your sector, there are most likely to be a number of cloud-based applications which fulfil a purpose specific to your industry.

For example, in the golf club sector, cloud-based apps record and monitor members handicaps and attendance, in recruitment a number of applications allow for candidate tracking and submission of documentation, estate agents have their own set of available specific applications designed to help putting properties on the market and track deals. In fact, there are but a handful of industries which aren't touched by having a cloud-based application designed to help those working in their sector.

Within this you'll also find function-specific cloud applications tailored not to a specific industry but a function of a business, such as sales, marketing, and accountancy (already touched on above with Xero and Sage). In the sales function, applications such as Salesforce.com keep a track on deals, opportunities and cases, in the marketing arena the likes of Hubspot automates marketing activity.

When I speak to businesses who state they are already using cloud applications, they will most often be using these sector-specific applications. Although the applications help them deliver a better experience for their customers and helps them work more effectively, they do not provide a complete cloud solution. They will most often still be using email services and require files to be stored on desktops within the office. Even though they are using some cloud applications, they still require local infrastructure which, again, suffers from all the issues outlined above: it requires management, back-up and needs to be maintained regularly, which involves regular upgrades, updates and new licences. A true cloud solution takes away all this pain.

These applications aren't designed to provide a complete end-to-end solution, incorporating email, document storage, accounting and everything else expected within a busy office.

All-purpose cloud-based applications or services

Now, we're moving into the realm of cloud-based applications designed to fulfil a range of needs within an office or business.

Into this category, you can add Google Apps, Microsoft 365 and upstarts such as Zoho, all of which offer the full suite of business applications from email to word processing, project management, contacts management, CRM, spreadsheet and other applications.

The benefits of these all-purpose applications is clear. Every need is catered for within your business and because every user is operating in a cloud environment, it makes the process of sharing and collaborating much easier.

It adds resilience to your business - effectively no-one is tied to a physical computer or laptop - so no disaster or office-based problem can cause a halt to productivity. Growth is possible (as well as downscaling if needed) as these are operated on a per user basis and the flexibility allows you to add people quickly as and when you need them.

In Google Docs, for example, you are even able to collaborate in real-time with several users working on a document at the same time with changes made immediately on-screen.

These services also benefit from being cost-effective compared with alternative offline options, such as Microsoft Office.

The main drawback to all-purpose services is their lack of flexibility and your lack of control over data (see specifically the USA PATRIOT Act section below).

Migrating your business to one of these all-purpose cloud services is less about migrating and more about changing how you previously worked. If you are used to working a certain way, unfortunately these systems offer you a very limited degree of flexibility.

There is a great deal of control over user access and with what is shared with who, but very little control over the way applications work with each other and how you can store and arrange you content within the application. For the most part, you'll also find there is a limit to how much functionality some services offer, compared with their offline options.

Fully managed cloud-based solutions

It's at this end of the market where businesses begin to see huge benefits from moving to the cloud.

A fully managed hosted solution allows a business to operate a system with none of the traditional problems associated with an in-house IT set-up.

There is no need for an in-house server and every element of the set-up is managed off-site by a dedicated team available at the other end of the phone.

While it delivers all the same benefits as less managed cloud providers, including resilience, automatic back-up, flexibility and cost-effectiveness, it also has a major advantage over the big tech brand all-purpose solutions: it can be moulded to your existing business systems *if* - and that's a <u>big</u> if - you choose the right cloud computing provider.

The worst possible situation is migrating to a platform which users within an entire organisation have to 'get used to'.

In my opinion, technology is not there to get in the way. Technology should be designed to facilitate our businesses and help us grow. Being able to enjoy a system which fits with what you need as business and in the form you need it is essential, not just to ensure there is no break in service, but for this simple fact: you know how best to run your business.

You know exactly what needs to happen and how to make customers come back, spend money and leave happy.

Why should you be dictated to by a technology company as to how you should run your business?

You shouldn't. Your system is there for you and it needs to be set-up according to your business's specific and individual needs.

You may also require specific third-party applications which, if you are using 'closed' all purpose cloud solutions, may simply not be compatible or unavailable.

And, of course, choosing the right hosted solution provider should also allow you to mix in the industry, sector or function specific cloud based applications too.

Why not all cloud computing providers/remote desktop providers are the same

For businesses going down the fully managed route, finding a cloud provider isn't difficult.

Search Google and you'll find lists and lists of companies offering to help you join the cloud computing revolution. Many of these businesses will have been traditional IT support companies who have helped migrate their customers into the cloud, while others will be cloud-specific start-ups jumping into the market to cash in on the revolution which is upon us or are even white labelling other providers' solutions.

The process is more complex than simply choosing a 'good' cloud computing provider; you need to choose the 'right' cloud computing provider for the specific needs of your business.

The first step is understanding what you need in a company offering cloud computing solutions. This is particularly important as you'll need to strategise what you are doing now and what your needs may be for the future.

Are you a company going through a period of stability or are you experiencing rapid growth?

Do you know what your needs are going to be in three months, 12 months or five years?

With this in mind, it's worth noting cloud service are defined by their cost, flexibility and ability to scale. Most good services operate on a per user, per application basis so you only pay for what you need, when you need it.

The next step is to consider your existing situation and how fixed your current business systems are and how much you would be willing to change how you work to fit round a cloud computing provider's system.

A common trait of many of the cloud-based applications in the market is their standardised approach. The stability and reliability of applications is a necessity to ensure their use across a global market; the problem with this situation is the lack of flexibility in moulding the use of these applications to your own system.

Even with managed cloud providers, there is a huge difference in the level of customisation they are able or willing to deliver. It is imperative checks are made beforehand that a cloud computing provider for your business has previous experience of successful migrations into businesses which have bespoke or tailored needs.

For instance, in my own business we have migrated business from sectors diverse as accountancy and estate agency through to retail and factory engineering. In each case, we were able to create a hosted cloud solution for their business which mirrored their existing set-up exactly. When those businesses' users opened their desktops and logged-in the day after migration, everything looked exactly the same as from before the migration. Shared drives were in the same place, folders and files were organised according to how they had always been organised.

From a user perspective, nothing had changed in terms of their workflow. This means zero downtime, no time wasted to re-learn how to use a new system and the opportunity to carry on working as if nothing had happened (but with all the added benefits of managed cloud hosting).

Above I mentioned a lack of understanding about migration and how to manage the process effectively was a major barrier to adoption. However, it isn't the biggest. That accolade falls to concerns about security.

While the perception is that cloud computing poses a security threat, generally your data has never been safer.

Which is better - a server in your office containing all your sensitive data or your data stored off-site in a Tier Four Aligned data centre manned 24/7 with security built-in? Put this way, the answer is clear.

However, there is one huge caveat to this security issue which has caused something of a storm in the cloud market in recent years. And it starts with a question: do you *really* know how safe your data is?

Global vs UK - a warning from National Security Agency and the USA PATRIOT Act

One of - if not the greatest - concerns which remains an obstacles for businesses wishing to migrate their IT to the cloud is security. According to a 2014 survey, the largest barrier to adoption of cloud services amongst potential businesses looking to make the jump was security and, specifically, data hosting.

The hosting of cloud services by any particular cloud provider may be in a country different from that in which they are based. In fact, some providers will operate data centres all over the world and so any data they host may be distributed in data centres in various locations. They may even be unaware of where data is.

While this is done for reasons of cost-effectiveness and resilience, it also brings up a serious issue in terms of jurisdiction and in particular a piece of legislation called the USA PATRIOT Act.

As evidenced in the case of Edward Snowden, the Act gives the US government and its agencies far-reaching powers to call up and monitor data on all businesses either based within the US or operating on US soil. This means any data centre in the US is subject to the Act as well as any data centre based outside of the US if it is owned by a US-based company.

This discovery has caused shockwaves. In Europe, where these all-invasive powers are seriously frowned upon, there is now widespread uncertainty and concern about using US cloud-based services and services with data centres based in the US.

From a business perspective, it also means something more fundamental. Even if you are using a service such as Dropbox or Gmail, you are subject to the Act and potentially your personal data can be viewed.

As an individual this may not mean too much from your own perspective. However, as a business how comfortable are you telling your clients and customers you cannot 100% guarantee their data won't be subject to these invasive laws?

If you are considering using a US-based service or a cloud provider who uses data centres based in the US, then seriously consider these implications.

The problem is, it's not easy to find out whether they do. In the UK, there are many cloud providers who simply white label another providers' solution. Businesses who believe they have contracted with a UK firm often end up hosted on services outside the UK. A little digging helps resolve this issue.

By way of example, at Worknet our data centres are based in the UK so we know our client data is not subject to the Act. We also own all the equipment, so we know exactly where our customers' data is and have the confidence in its security.

DOWNLOAD - Want to discover more about how your data may be subject to prying eyes? Go to www.worknet.co.uk/patriotact to download the free guide *How safe is your data? A guide to the USA PATRIOT Act*.

A Cloud Computing provider checklist

Find the right provider for your business

In order to fully assess how you will be best served by the cloud computing options available to you, it is recommended you first assess your IT business needs.

To help this process, here is a checklist by which you can properly assess and identify the needs of your business from your IT network. This is, by no means, an exhaustive list and the nature of your business will likely dictate the emphasis placed on areas of specific need, such as security or flexibility. However, hopefully this list should represent a starting point in your consideration of the issues.

Consider each of these questions:

What is your level of risk?

What risks does your immediate physical environment pose? Consider environmental, social and political.

What is the nature of the information you are storing?

Are you storing confidential or sensitive client data? Or do you just need it for internal purposes? How regularly do you need to back-up? How far back would you need to go to recover?

What will the business need this year? Next year? And beyond?

Do you need to build scalability into your solution? Can you afford to constantly upgrade your server every few years or would it make sense making the investment now?

How much flexibility do you require?

Do you have any staff outside the office? How often do they need to work outside the office? Do you have plans to add home workers or build flexibility into the way you work?

What level of SLA do you require?

Check the terms carefully to ensure you are happy with the level of service being provided. Response times of 24 hours (which can often mean three working days according to some small print) may seem acceptable, but when your business is out for this length of time the reality of not having support available within a few hours hits home.

What happens if I need to move?

How easy is it to move my data should I need to change provider? What happens if the cloud services providers goes out of business? Is there a system in place where I can recover my data in these eventualities? Will I be charged?

An offer

How to guarantee the success of your business's cloud computing platform

If you are seriously interested in making the move to the cloud and all the benefits it brings, including:

- Improved resilience and disaster recovery built in should the unthinkable happen

- Greater flexibility to work from home, from client offices or even on holiday

- Enhanced security to protect your sensitive customer data and confidential company information

- Unlimited scaleability to protect your investment in your IT infrastructure and grow your business as fast or as slow as you need to.

Then, I would like to make you an offer to join the cloud computing revolution and watch your business soar in 2015.

The biggest obstacle to making the leap to cloud computing is the unknown and not knowing whether it'll work in your business. So let me help you take away this uncertainty.

Choose from one of Worknet's plans and try it for a month.

If you don't like it - and you don't experience the incredible difference it makes to your business - we'll reinstall all your data back on your server as though nothing had happened.

And you won't owe us a penny.

To experience the benefits of cloud computing for your business, call one of my team today on 01628 563636 and quote 'Book offer'.

Printed in Great Britain
by Amazon.co.uk, Ltd.,
Marston Gate.